Cram101 Textbook Outlines to accompany:

Sexuality Now: Embracing Diversity

Janell L. Carroll, 3rd Edition

A Content Technologies Inc. publication (c) 2012.

Cram101 Textbook Outlines and Cram101.com are Cram101 Inc. publications and services. All notes, highlights, reviews, and practice tests are written and prepared by Content Technologies and Cram101, all rights reserved.

WHY STOP HERE... THERE'S MORE ONLINE

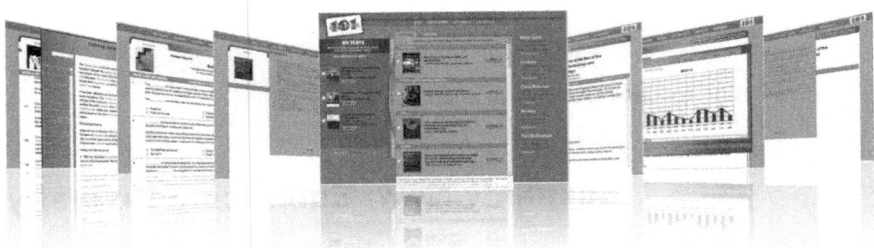

With technology and experience, we've developed tools that make studying easier and efficient. Like this Cram101 textbook notebook, Cram101.com offers you the highlights from every chapter of your actual textbook. However, unlike this notebook, Cram101.com gives you practice tests for each of the chapters. You also get access to in-depth reference material for writing essays and papers.

By purchasing this book, you get 50% off the normal subscription free!. Just enter the promotional code **'DK73DW13451'** on the Cram101.com registration screen.

CRAM101.COM FEATURES:

Outlines & Highlights
Just like the ones in this notebook, but with links to additional information.

Integrated Note Taking
Add your class notes to the Cram101 notes, print them and maximize your study time.

Problem Solving
Step-by-step walk throughs for math, stats and other disciplines.

Practice Exams
Five different test taking formats for every chapter.

Easy Access
Study any of your books, on any computer, anywhere.

Unlimited Textbooks
All the features above for virtually all your textbooks, just add them to your account at no additional cost.

TRY THE FIRST CHAPTER FREE!

Be sure to use the promo code above when registering on Cram101.com to get 50% off your membership fees.

STUDYING MADE EASY

This Cram101 notebook is designed to make studying easier and increase your comprehension of the textbook material. Instead of starting with a blank notebook and trying to write down everything discussed in class lectures, you can use this Cram101 textbook notebook and annotate your notes along with the lecture.

Our goal is to give you the best tools for success.

For a supreme understanding of the course, pair your notebook with our online tools. Should you decide you prefer Cram101.com as your study tool,

we'd like to offer you a trade...

Our Trade In program is a simple way for us to keep our promise and provide you the best studying tools, regardless of where you purchased your Cram101 textbook notebook. As long as your notebook is in *Like New Condition**, you can send it back to us and we will immediately give you a Cram101.com account free for 120 days!

Let The **Trade In** Begin!

THREE SIMPLE STEPS TO TRADE:

1. Go to www.cram101.com/tradein and fill out the packing slip information.

2. Submit and print the packing slip and mail it in with your Cram101 textbook notebook.

3. Activate your account after you receive your email confirmation.

---

* Books must be returned in *Like New Condition*, meaning there is no damage to the book including, but not limited to; ripped or torn pages, markings or writing on pages, or folded / creased pages. Upon receiving the book, Cram101 will inspect it and reserves the right to terminate your free Cram101.com account and return your textbook notebook at the owners expense.

Learning System

Cram101 Textbook Outlines is a learning system. The notes in this book are the highlights of your textbook, you will never have to highlight a book again.

How to use this book. Take this book to class, it is your notebook for the lecture. The notes and highlights on the left hand side of the pages follow the outline and order of the textbook. All you have to do is follow along while your instructor presents the lecture. Circle the items emphasized in class and add other important information on the right side. With Cram101 Textbook Outlines you'll spend less time writing and more time listening. Learning becomes more efficient.

Cram101.com Online

Increase your studying efficiency by using Cram101.com's practice tests and online reference material. It is the perfect complement to Cram101 Textbook Outlines. Use self-teaching matching tests or simulate in-class testing with comprehensive multiple choice tests, or simply use Cram's true and false tests for quick review. Cram101.com even allows you to enter your in-class notes for an integrated studying format combining the textbook notes with your class notes.

Visit **www.Cram101.com**, click Sign Up at the top of the screen, and enter **DK73DW13451** in the promo code box on the registration screen. Your access to www.Cram101.com is discounted by 50% because you have purchased this book. Sign up and stop highlighting textbooks forever.

Copyright © 2011 by Cram101, Inc. All rights reserved. "Cram101"® and "Never Highlight a Book Again!"® are registered trademarks of Cram101, Inc. ISBN(s): 1428898239. PUBR-5.2011311

Sexuality Now: Embracing Diversity
Janell L. Carroll, 3rd

CONTENTS

1. Exploring Human Sexuality: Past and Present 2
2. Understanding Human Sexuality: Theory and Research 8
3. Communication: Enriching Your Sexuality 20
4. Gender Development, Gender Roles, and Gender Identity 22
5. Female Sexual Anatomy and Physiology 32
6. Male Sexual Anatomy and Physiology 38
7. Love and Intimacy 42
8. Childhood and Adolescent Sexuality 48
9. Adult Sexual Relationships 54
10. Sexual Expression: Arousal and Response 62
11. Sexual Orientation 68
12. Pregnancy and Birth 78
13. Contraception and Abortion 84
14. Challenges to Sexual Functioning 92
15. Sexually Transmitted Infections and HIV/AIDS 98
16. Varieties of Sexual Expression 102
17. Power and Sexual Coercion 110
18. Sexual Images and Selling Sex 120

Chapter 1. Exploring Human Sexuality: Past and Present

Abortion	Abortion is the termination of a pregnancy by the removal or expulsion of a fetus or embryo from the uterus, resulting in or caused by its death. An abortion can occur spontaneously due to complications during pregnancy or can be induced, in humans and other species. In the context of human pregnancies, an abortion induced to preserve the health of the gravida (pregnant female) is termed a therapeutic abortion, while an abortion induced for any other reason is termed an elective abortion.
Phallus	A phallus is an erect penis, a penis-shaped object such as a dildo, or a mimetic image of an erect penis. Any object that symbolically resembles a penis may also be referred to as a phallus; however, such objects are more often referred to as being phallic (as in "phallic symbol"). Such symbols often represent the fertility and cultural implications that are associated with the male sexual organ, as well as the male orgasm.
Pederasty	Pederasty is a (usually erotic) relationship between an older man and an adolescent boy outside his immediate family. Historically, pederasty has existed as a variety of customs and practices within different cultures. The status of pederasty has changed over the course of history, at times considered an ideal and at other times a crime.
Celibacy	Celibacy refers to a state of not being married, or a state of abstention from sexual intercourse or vow of marriage. This word derives from two Proto-Indo-European stems, *kaiwelo- "alone" and *lib(h)s- "living". Abstinence and celibacy The words abstinence and celibacy are often used interchangeably, but are different.
Chastity	Chastity is sexual behavior of a man or woman acceptable to the moral norms and guidelines of a culture, civilization, or religion.

Chapter 1. Exploring Human Sexuality: Past and Present

Chapter 1. Exploring Human Sexuality: Past and Present

	In the western world, the term has become closely associated (and is often used interchangeably) with sexual abstinence, especially before marriage. However, the term remains applicable to persons in all states, single or married, clerical or lay, and has implications beyond sexual temperance.
Cognitive dissonance	Cognitive dissonance is an uncomfortable feeling caused by holding conflicting ideas simultaneously. The theory of cognitive dissonance proposes that people have a motivational drive to reduce dissonance. They do this by changing their attitudes, beliefs, and actions.
Bundling	Bundling, was the traditional practice of wrapping one person in a bed accompanied by another, usually as a part of courting behavior. The tradition is thought to have originated either in the Netherlands or in the British Isles and later became common in Colonial America, especially in Pennsylvania Dutch Country. When used for courtship, the aim was to allow intimacy without sexual intercourse.
Slavery	Slavery is a system under which people are treated as property and are forced to work. Slaves can be held against their will from the time of their capture, purchase or birth, and deprived of the right to leave, to refuse to work, or to demand compensation. In some historical situations it has been legal for owners to kill slaves.
Free love	Origin The term free love has been used since at least the 19th century to describe a social movement that rejects marriage, which is seen as a form of social bondage, especially for women. The Free Love movement's initial goal was to separate the state from sexual matters such as marriage, birth control, and adultery. It claimed that such issues were the concern of the people involved, and no one else.
Cancer	Cancer (medical term: malignant neoplasm) is a class of diseases in which a group of cells display uncontrolled growth, invasion that intrudes upon and destroys adjacent tissues, and sometimes metastasis, or spreading to other locations in the body via lymph or blood. These three malignant properties of cancers differentiate them from benign tumors, which do not invade or metastasize.

Chapter 1. Exploring Human Sexuality: Past and Present

Chapter 1. Exploring Human Sexuality: Past and Present

	Researchers divide the causes of cancer into two groups: those with an environmental cause and those with a hereditary genetic cause.
Feminism	Feminism refers to movements aimed at defining, establishing and defending equal political, economic, and social rights and equal opportunities for women. Its concepts overlap with those of women's rights. Feminism is mainly focused on women's issues, but because feminism seeks gender equality, some feminists argue that men's liberation is therefore a necessary part of feminism, and that men are also harmed by sexism and gender roles.

Chapter 1. Exploring Human Sexuality: Past and Present

Chapter 2. Understanding Human Sexuality: Theory and Research

Libido	Libido in its common usage means sexual desire; however more technical definitions, such as those found in the work of Carl Jung, are more general, referring to libido as the free creative--or psychic--energy an individual has to put toward personal development or individuation. Within the category of sexual behavior, libido would fall under the appetitive phase wherein an individual will usually undergo certain behaviors in order to gain access to a mate. History of the concept Sigmund Freud popularized the term and defined libido as the instinct energy or force, contained in what Freud called the id, the largely unconscious structure of the psyche.
Psychoanalytic theory	Psychoanalytic theory refers to the definition and dynamics of personality development which underlie and guide psychoanalytic and psychodynamic psychotherapy. First laid out by Sigmund Freud, psychoanalytic theory has undergone many refinements since his work. Psychoanalytic theory came to full prominence as a critical force in the last third of the twentieth century as part of 'the flow of critical discourse after the 1960s', and in association above all with the name of Jacques Lacan.
BDSM	BDSM is a consensual lifestyle choice, or type of adult roleplay between two or more individuals. The compound acronym, BDSM, is derived from the terms bondage and discipline (B'D), dominance and submission (D's), sadism and masochism (S'M) BDSM includes a wide spectrum of activities, forms of interpersonal relationships, and distinct subcultures. Activities and relationships within a BDSM context are characterized by the fact that the participants usually take on complementary, but unequal roles, thus the idea of consent of both the partners becomes essential.

Chapter 2. Understanding Human Sexuality: Theory and Research

Chapter 2. Understanding Human Sexuality: Theory and Research

Oedipus complex	In psychoanalytic theory, the term Oedipus complex denotes the emotions and ideas that the mind keeps in the unconscious, via dynamic repression, that concentrate upon a boy's desire to sexually possess his mother, and kill his father. In the course of his psychosexual development, the complex is the boy's phallic stage formation of a discrete sexual identity; a girl's analogous experience is the Electra complex. The Oedipus complex occurs in the third -- phallic stage (ages 3-6) -- of five psychosexual development stages: (i) the Oral, (ii) the Anal, (iii) the Phallic, (iv) the Latent, and (v) the Genital -- in which the source libido pleasure is in a different erogenous zone of the infant's body.
Anal stage	The anal stage, in Freudian psychology, is the period of human development occurring at about one to two years of age. Around this age, the child begins to toilet train, which brings about the child's fascination in the erogenous zone of the anus. The anal stage coincides with the start of the child's ability to control his anal sphincter, and therefore his ability to give or withhold gifts at will.
Fixation	Fixation: concept originated by Sigmund Freud (1905a) to denote the persistence of anachronistic sexual traits'. Subsequently '"Fixation" acquired a broader connotation. With the development of theory of libidinal stages...the term came to mean a persistent attachment, not only to the specific instinctual aims of a particular era, but, instead, to the entire complex of self and object relation' at that time.
Genital stage	The genital stage in psychology is the term used by Sigmund Freud to describe the final stage of human psychosexual development. This stage begins at the start of puberty when sexual urges are once again awakened. Through the lessons learned during the previous stages, adolescents direct their sexual urges onto opposite sex peers, with the primary focus of pleasure of the genitals.
Latency	Latency is a concept in political science referring to existent political opinions that have yet to be fully expressed. Leaders may arouse latent opinions and convert them into political action.
Latency stage	In his model of the child's psychosexual development, Sigmund Freud describes five stages. Freud believed that the child discharges his/her libido (sexual energy) through a distinct body area that characterizes each stage.

Chapter 2. Understanding Human Sexuality: Theory and Research

Chapter 2. Understanding Human Sexuality: Theory and Research

The stages are:

- the 'oral phase' (first stage)
- the 'anal phase' (second stage)
- the 'phallic phase' (third stage)
- the 'latency phase' (fourth stage)
- the 'genital phase' (fifth stage).

Because the latency stage is less of a stage and more of period between stages, it may begin at any time between the ages of 3 and 7 (whenever the child goes to school) and may continue until anywhere from the ages of 8 to 13 (whenever the child's puberty begins).

Oral stage — In Freudian psychoanalysis, the term oral stage denotes the first psychosexual development stage wherein the mouth of the infant is his or her primary erogenous zone. Spanning the life period from birth to the age of 21 months, the oral stage is the first of the five Freudian psychosexual development stages: (i) the Oral, (ii) the Anal, (iii) the Phallic, (iv) the Latent, and (v) the Genital. Moreover, because it is the infant's first human relationship -- biological (nutritive) and psychological (emotional) -- its duration depends upon the child-rearing mores of the mother's society.

Phallic stage — In Freudian psychology, the Phallic stage is the third stage of psychosexual development, spanning the ages of three to six years, wherein the infant's libido (desire) centers upon his or her genitalia as the erogenous zone. When children become aware of their bodies, the bodies of other children, and the bodies of their parents, they gratify physical curiosity by undressing and exploring each other and their genitals, the center of the phallic stage, in course of which they learn the physical differences between "male" and "female", and the gender differences between "boy" and "girl", experiences which alter the psychologic dynamics of the parent and child relationship. The phallic stage is the third of five Freudian psychosexual development stages: (i) the Oral, (ii) the Anal, (iii) the Phallic, (iv) the Latent, and (v) the Genital.

Chapter 2. Understanding Human Sexuality: Theory and Research

Chapter 2. Understanding Human Sexuality: Theory and Research

Psychoanalysis	Psychoanalysis is a body of ideas developed by Austrian neurologist Sigmund Freud and continued by others. It is primarily devoted to the study of human psychological functioning and behavior, although it can also be applied to societies. Psychoanalysis has three main components: 1. a method of investigation of the mind and the way one thinks; 2. a systematized set of theories about human behavior; 3. a method of treatment of psychological or emotional illness. Under the broad umbrella of psychoanalysis, there are at least 22 theoretical orientations regarding human mentation and development.
Cognitive switch theory	Cognitive switch theory is a theory in gender role awareness. This theory states that all children are born neutral; sex is there but gender is not. The child thereafter becomes deliberate in filtering information that is biased toward the gender they believe they are.
Social learning theory	Social learning theory is the theory that people learn new behavior through observational learning of the social factors in their environment. If people observe positive, desired outcomes in the observed behavior, then they are more likely to model, imitate, and adopt the behavior themselves. Modern theory is closely associated with Julian Rotter and Albert Bandura.
Therapy	Therapy is the attempted remediation of a health problem, usually following a diagnosis. In the medical field, it is synonymous with the word "treatment". Among psychologists, the term may refer specifically to psychotherapy or "talk therapy".
Love	Love is the emotion of strong affection and personal attachment. In philosophical context, love is a virtue representing all of human kindness, compassion, and affection. In some religious contexts, love is not just a virtue, but the basis for all being, as in the Roman Catholic phrase, "God is love".
Self-actualization	Self-actualization is a term that has been used in various psychology theories, often in slightly different ways. The term was originally introduced by the organismic theorist Kurt Goldstein for the motive to realize one's full potential. In his view, it is the organism's master motive, the only real motive: 'the tendency to actualize itself as fully as possible is the basic drive...the drive of self-actualization'.

Chapter 2. Understanding Human Sexuality: Theory and Research

Chapter 2. Understanding Human Sexuality: Theory and Research

Feminist theory	Feminist theory is the extension of feminism into theoretical, or philosophical discourse, it aims to understand the nature of gender inequality. It examines women's social roles and lived experience, and feminist politics in a variety of fields, such as anthropology and sociology, psychoanalysis, economics, literary criticism, and philosophy. While generally providing a critique of social relations, much of feminist theory also focuses on analyzing gender inequality and the promotion of women's rights, interests, and issues.
Queer	Queer is an umbrella term for sexual minorities that are not heterosexual, heteronormative, or gender-binary. In the context of Western identity politics the term also acts as a label setting queer-identifying people apart from discourse, ideologies, and lifestyles that typify mainstream LGBT (lesbian, gay, bisexual, and transsexual) communities as being oppressive or assimilationist. This term is controversial because it was reappropriated only two decades ago from its use as an anti-gay epithet.
Queer theory	Queer theory is a field of critical theory that emerged in the early 1990s out of the fields of LGBT studies and feminist studies. It is a kind of interpretation devoted to queer readings of texts. Heavily influenced by the work of Jacob Edwards, queer theory builds both upon feminist challenges to the idea that gender is part of the essential self and upon gay/lesbian studies' close examination of the socially constructed nature of sexual acts and identities.
Rape	In criminal law, rape is a type of sexual assault usually involving sexual intercourse, which is initiated by one or more persons against another person without that person's consent. According to the American Medical Association (1995), sexual violence, and rape in particular, is considered the most under-reported violent crime. The rate of reporting, prosecution and convictions for rape varies considerably in different jurisdictions.

Chapter 2. Understanding Human Sexuality:Theory and Research

Chapter 2. Understanding Human Sexuality: Theory and Research

Homosexuality	Homosexuality is romantic and/or sexual attraction or behavior among members of the same sex or gender. As a sexual orientation, homosexuality refers to "an enduring pattern of or disposition to experience sexual, affectional, or romantic attractions" primarily or exclusively to people of the same sex; "it also refers to an individual's sense of personal and social identity based on those attractions, behaviors expressing them, and membership in a community of others who share them."
Dependant	A dependant is a person who relies on another as a primary source of income. For example, a minor child, under the age of majority, is a dependant of his or her parent and the existence of the dependant may enable the provider, such as a parent or guardian, to claim a deduction, for example in income tax calculations.
AIDS	Acquired immune deficiency syndrome or acquired immunodeficiency syndrome (AIDS) is a disease of the human immune system caused by the human immunodeficiency virus (HIV). This condition progressively reduces the effectiveness of the immune system and leaves individuals susceptible to opportunistic infections and tumors. HIV is transmitted through direct contact of a mucous membrane or the bloodstream with a bodily fluid containing HIV, such as blood, semen, vaginal fluid, preseminal fluid, and breast milk.

Chapter 2. Understanding Human Sexuality: Theory and Research

Chapter 3. Communication: Enriching Your Sexuality

Communication	Communication is a process whereby meaning is defined and shared between living organisms. Communication requires a sender, a message, and an intended recipient, although the receiver need not be present or aware of the sender's intent to communicate at the time of communication; thus communication can occur across vast distances in time and space. Communication requires that the communicating parties share an area of communicative commonality.
Sexual orientation	Sexual orientation describes a pattern of emotional, romantic, or sexual attraction to men, women, both genders, neither gender, or another gender. According to the American Psychological Association, sexual orientation is enduring and also refers to a person's sense of "personal and social identity based on those attractions, behaviors expressing them, and membership in a community of others who share them." The consensus among most contemporary scholars in the field is that one's sexual orientation is not a choice. No simple, single cause for sexual orientation has been conclusively demonstrated, but research suggests that it is by a combination of genetic, hormonal, and environmental influences, with biological factors involving a complex interplay of genetic factors and the early uterine environment.
Social network	A social network is a social structure made up of individuals (or organizations) called "nodes", which are tied (connected) by one or more specific types of interdependency, such as friendship, kinship, common interest, financial exchange, dislike, sexual relationships, or relationships of beliefs, knowledge or prestige. Social network analysis views social relationships in terms of network theory consisting of nodes and ties (also called edges, links, or connections). Nodes are the individual actors within the networks, and ties are the relationships between the actors.
Active listening	Active listening is a communication technique that requires the listener to understand, interpret, and evaluate what he hears. The ability to listen actively can improve personal relationships through reducing conflicts, strengthening cooperation, and fostering understanding. When interacting, people often are not listening attentively.

Chapter 3. Communication: Enriching Your Sexuality

Chapter 4. Gender Development, Gender Roles, and Gender Identity

Gonad	The gonad is the organ that makes gametes. The gonads in males are the testicles and the gonads in females are the ovaries. The product, gametes, are haploid germ cells.
BDSM	BDSM is a consensual lifestyle choice, or type of adult roleplay between two or more individuals. The compound acronym, BDSM, is derived from the terms bondage and discipline (B'D), dominance and submission (D's), sadism and masochism (S'M)
	BDSM includes a wide spectrum of activities, forms of interpersonal relationships, and distinct subcultures.
	Activities and relationships within a BDSM context are characterized by the fact that the participants usually take on complementary, but unequal roles, thus the idea of consent of both the partners becomes essential.
Menopause	Menopause is a term used to describe the permanent cessation of the primary functions of the human ovaries: the ripening and release of ova and the release of hormones that cause both the creation of the uterine lining and the subsequent shedding of the uterine lining (a.k.a. the menses). Menopause typically (but not always) occurs in women in midlife, during their late 40s or early 50s, and signals the end of the fertile phase of a woman's life.
Testosterone	Testosterone is a steroid hormone from the androgen group and is found in mammals, reptiles, birds, and other vertebrates. In mammals, testosterone is primarily secreted in the testes of males and the ovaries of females, although small amounts are also secreted by the adrenal glands. It is the principal male sex hormone and an anabolic steroid.
Sex organ	A sex organ, as narrowly defined, is any of the anatomical parts of the body which are involved in sexual reproduction and constitute the reproductive system in a complex organism; flowers are the reproductive organs of flowering plants, cones are the reproductive organs of coniferous plants, whereas mosses, ferns, and other similar plants have gametangia for reproductive organs.

Chapter 4. Gender Development, Gender Roles, and Gender Identity

Chapter 4. Gender Development, Gender Roles, and Gender Identity

Turner syndrome	Turner syndrome encompasses several conditions, of which monosomy X (absence of an entire sex chromosome, the Barr body) is most common. It is a chromosomal abnormality in which all or part of one of the sex chromosomes is absent (unaffected humans have 46 chromosomes, of which two are sex chromosomes). Typical females have two X chromosomes, but in Turner syndrome, one of those sex chromosomes is missing or has other abnormalities.
Congenital adrenal hyperplasia	Congenital adrenal hyperplasia refers to any of several autosomal recessive diseases resulting from mutations of genes for enzymes mediating the biochemical steps of production of cortisol from cholesterol by the adrenal glands (steroidogenesis). Most of these conditions involve excessive or deficient production of sex steroids and can alter development of primary or secondary sex characteristics in some affected infants, children, or adults. Congenital adrenal hyperplasia is one of the possible underlying synthesis problems in Addison's disease.
Hermaphrodite	In biology, a hermaphrodite is a plant or animal that has reproductive organs normally associated with both male and female sexes. Many taxonomic groups of animals (mostly invertebrates) do not have separate sexes. In these groups, hermaphroditism is a normal condition, enabling a form of sexual reproduction in which both partners can act as the "female" or "male".
Therapy	Therapy is the attempted remediation of a health problem, usually following a diagnosis. In the medical field, it is synonymous with the word "treatment". Among psychologists, the term may refer specifically to psychotherapy or "talk therapy".
Luteinizing hormone	Luteinizing hormone is a hormone produced by the anterior pituitary gland. In females, an acute rise of luteinizing hormone called the luteinizing hormone surge triggers ovulation and development of the corpus luteum. In males, where luteinizing hormone had also been called interstitial cell-stimulating hormone (ICSH), it stimulates Leydig cell production of testosterone.
Oxytocin	Oxytocin is a mammalian hormone that acts primarily as a neuromodulator in the brain. Also known as alpha-hypophamine (α-hypophamine), oxytocin has the distinction of being the very first polypeptide hormone to be sequenced and synthesized biochemically, by Vincent du Vigneaud et al. in 1953.

Chapter 4. Gender Development, Gender Roles, and Gender Identity

Chapter 4. Gender Development, Gender Roles, and Gender Identity

Cancer	Cancer (medical term: malignant neoplasm) is a class of diseases in which a group of cells display uncontrolled growth, invasion that intrudes upon and destroys adjacent tissues, and sometimes metastasis, or spreading to other locations in the body via lymph or blood. These three malignant properties of cancers differentiate them from benign tumors, which do not invade or metastasize. Researchers divide the causes of cancer into two groups: those with an environmental cause and those with a hereditary genetic cause.
Femininity	Femininity refers to female qualities attributed specifically to women and girls. The complement to femininity is masculinity. Feminine traits are often associated with life-giving and nurturing qualities of elegance, gentleness, motherhood, birth, intuition, creativity, life-death-rebirth and biological life cycle. The feminine archetype in mythology and world religion, is associated with a natural creative force that has a feminine or maternal function such as Mother Nature, Mother Earth, Great Mother, Great Goddess, and Mitochondrial Eve.
Gender role	Gender roles refers to the set of social and behavioral norms that are widely considered to be socially appropriate for individuals of a specific sex in the context of a specific culture, which differ widely between cultures and over time. There are differences of opinion as to whether observed gender differences in behavior and personality characteristics are, at least in part, due to cultural or social factors, and therefore, the product of socialization experiences, or to what extent gender differences are due to biological and physiological differences. Though some views on gender-based differentiation in the workplace and in interpersonal relationships has undergone profound changes, especially in Western countries, as a result of feminist influences, there are still considerable differences in gender roles in almost all societies.
Masculinity	Masculinity is, according The American Heritage Dictionary, someone or something that posses characteristics normally associated with males. The term can be used to describe any human, animal or object that has the quality of being masculine. When masculine is used to describe men, it can have degrees of comparison--more masculine, most masculine.

Chapter 4. Gender Development, Gender Roles, and Gender Identity

Chapter 4. Gender Development, Gender Roles, and Gender Identity

Wet nurse	A wet nurse is a woman hired to breast feed and care for another's child. Wet nurses are hired when the mother is unable or chooses not to nurse the child herself. Wet-nursed children may be known as "milk-siblings", and in some cultures the families are linked by a special relationship of milk kinship.
Drag	Drag is used for any clothing carrying symbolic significance but usually referring to the clothing associated with one gender role when worn by a person of the other gender. The term may have originated in Athens, Greece in the fourth century BCE. when it was common practice for gender-nonconforming people to be dragged through the streets as punishment. The term "drag" may have been given a wider circulation in Polari, a gay street argot in England in the early part of the 20th century.
Queen	In gay slang, queen is a term used to refer to flamboyant or effeminate gay men. The term can either be pejorative, or celebrated as a type of self-identification. Related terms Drag queen A drag queen is a person, usually a man, who dresses, and usually acts, like a woman often for the purpose of entertaining or performing.
Transgenderism	Transgenderism is a social movement seeking transgender rights and affirming transgender pride. History In her 1995 book Apartheid of Sex, biopolitical lawyer and writer Martine Rothblatt describes "transgenderism" as a grassroots social movement seeking transgender rights and affirming transgender pride. For many in the transgender - or "trans" - movement, the label transgender encompasses not only transsexual and transgender people but also transvestites, drag queens, drag kings, intersex individuals, and anyone non-conventionally gendered (i.e., anyone identifying or behaving in a manner that runs counter to expected societal norms concerning the gender assigned them after birth) or sexed (if one includes transsexual people).

Chapter 4. Gender Development, Gender Roles, and Gender Identity

Chapter 4. Gender Development, Gender Roles, and Gender Identity

Transsexualism	Transsexualism is an individual's identification with a gender inconsistent or not culturally associated with their biological sex. A medical diagnosis can be made if a person experiences discomfort as a result of a desire to be a member of the opposite sex, or if a person experiences impaired functioning or distress as a result of that gender identification. Transsexualism is stigmatized in many parts of the world but has become more widely known in Western culture in the mid to late 20th century, concurrently with the sexual revolution and the development of sex reassignment surgery.
Third gender	The terms third gender and third sex describe individuals who are categorized (by their will or by social consensus) as neither male nor female, as well as the social category present in those societies who recognize three or more genders. The term "third" is usually understood to mean "other"; some anthropologists and sociologists have described fourth, fifth, and even some genders. Although biology determines genetically whether a human being is male, female (on the basis of the XX or XY or a variation thereof.
Asexuality	Asexuality in its broadest sense, is the lack of sexual attraction or the lack of interest in and desire for sex. Sometimes, it is considered a lack of a sexual orientation. One commonly cited study placed the prevalence of asexuality at 1%.
Play	"Play" is the term given to taking part in a BDSM scene. It is a deliberate use of the word's ambiguous meaning - suggesting both a Play in the literary sense (taking in the roleplay aspect) and Play in the child-like sense (taking in the experimentation, gleefullness and wonder aspects). Often in BDSM clubs, "Shall we play?" is the equivalent to the vanilla "Shall we dance?".

Chapter 4. Gender Development, Gender Roles, and Gender Identity

Chapter 5. Female Sexual Anatomy and Physiology

Sex organ	A sex organ, as narrowly defined, is any of the anatomical parts of the body which are involved in sexual reproduction and constitute the reproductive system in a complex organism; flowers are the reproductive organs of flowering plants, cones are the reproductive organs of coniferous plants, whereas mosses, ferns, and other similar plants have gametangia for reproductive organs.
Breastfeeding	Breastfeeding is the feeding of an infant or young child with breast milk directly from female human breasts (i.e., via lactation) rather than from a baby bottle or other container. Babies have a sucking reflex that enables them to suck and swallow milk. Most mothers can breastfeed for six months or more, without the addition of infant formula or solid food.
Oxytocin	Oxytocin is a mammalian hormone that acts primarily as a neuromodulator in the brain. Also known as alpha-hypophamine (α-hypophamine), oxytocin has the distinction of being the very first polypeptide hormone to be sequenced and synthesized biochemically, by Vincent du Vigneaud et al. in 1953.
Cancer	Cancer (medical term: malignant neoplasm) is a class of diseases in which a group of cells display uncontrolled growth, invasion that intrudes upon and destroys adjacent tissues, and sometimes metastasis, or spreading to other locations in the body via lymph or blood. These three malignant properties of cancers differentiate them from benign tumors, which do not invade or metastasize. Researchers divide the causes of cancer into two groups: those with an environmental cause and those with a hereditary genetic cause.
Puberty	Puberty is the process of physical changes by which a child's body becomes an adult body capable of reproduction. Puberty is initiated by hormone signals from the brain to the gonads (the ovaries and testes). In response, the gonads produce a variety of hormones that stimulate the growth, function, or transformation of brain, bones, muscle, blood, skin, hair, breasts, and sex organs. Growth accelerates in the first half of puberty and stops at the completion of puberty. Before puberty, body differences between boys and girls are almost entirely restricted to the genitalia. During puberty, major differences of size, shape, composition, and function develop in many body structures and systems. The most obvious of these are referred to as secondary sex characteristics.

Chapter 5. Female Sexual Anatomy and Physiology

Chapter 5. Female Sexual Anatomy and Physiology

Rape	In criminal law, rape is a type of sexual assault usually involving sexual intercourse, which is initiated by one or more persons against another person without that person's consent.
	According to the American Medical Association (1995), sexual violence, and rape in particular, is considered the most under-reported violent crime. The rate of reporting, prosecution and convictions for rape varies considerably in different jurisdictions.
Posttraumatic stress disorder	Posttraumatic stress disorder is a severe anxiety disorder that can develop after exposure to any event that results in psychological trauma. This event may involve the threat of death to oneself or to someone else, or to one's own or someone else's physical, sexual, or psychological integrity, overwhelming the individual's ability to cope. As an effect of psychological trauma, PTSD is less frequent and more enduring than the more commonly seen acute stress response.
Stress	Stress is a term in psychology and biology, first coined in the biological context in the 1930s, which has in more recent decades become commonly used in popular parlance. It refers to the consequence of the failure of an organism - human or animal - to respond appropriately to emotional or physical threats, whether actual or imagined.
	Signs of stress may be cognitive, emotional, physical or behavioral.
Menopause	Menopause is a term used to describe the permanent cessation of the primary functions of the human ovaries: the ripening and release of ova and the release of hormones that cause both the creation of the uterine lining and the subsequent shedding of the uterine lining (a.k.a. the menses). Menopause typically (but not always) occurs in women in midlife, during their late 40s or early 50s, and signals the end of the fertile phase of a woman's life.
Osteoporosis	Osteoporosis is a disease of bones that leads to an increased risk of fracture. In osteoporosis the bone mineral density (BMD) is reduced, bone microarchitecture is deteriorating, and the amount and variety of proteins in bone is altered. Osteoporosis is defined by the World Health Organization (WHO) as a bone mineral density that is 2.5 standard deviations or more below the mean peak bone mass (average of young, healthy adults) as measured by DXA; the term "established osteoporosis" includes the presence of a fragility fracture.

Chapter 5. Female Sexual Anatomy and Physiology

Chapter 5. Female Sexual Anatomy and Physiology

Therapy	Therapy is the attempted remediation of a health problem, usually following a diagnosis. In the medical field, it is synonymous with the word "treatment". Among psychologists, the term may refer specifically to psychotherapy or "talk therapy".
BDSM	BDSM is a consensual lifestyle choice, or type of adult roleplay between two or more individuals. The compound acronym, BDSM, is derived from the terms bondage and discipline (B'D), dominance and submission (D's), sadism and masochism (S'M)
	BDSM includes a wide spectrum of activities, forms of interpersonal relationships, and distinct subcultures.
	Activities and relationships within a BDSM context are characterized by the fact that the participants usually take on complementary, but unequal roles, thus the idea of consent of both the partners becomes essential.
Cervical cancer	Cervical cancer is malignant neoplasm of the cervix uteri or cervical area. It may present with vaginal bleeding, but symptoms may be absent until the cancer is in its advanced stages. Treatment consists of surgery (including local excision) in early stages and chemotherapy and radiotherapy in advanced stages of the disease.
Endometrial cancer	Endometrial cancer refers to several types of malignancies that arise from the endometrium, or lining, of the uterus. Endometrial cancers are the most common gynecologic cancers in the United States, with over 35,000 women diagnosed each year. The most common subtype, endometrioid adenocarcinoma, typically occurs within a few decades of menopause, is associated with excessive estrogen exposure, often develops in the setting of endometrial hyperplasia, and presents most often with vaginal bleeding.

Chapter 5. Female Sexual Anatomy and Physiology

Chapter 6. Male Sexual Anatomy and Physiology

Leydig cell	Leydig cells, also known as interstitial cells of Leydig, are found adjacent to the seminiferous tubules in the testicle. They produce testosterone in the presence of luteinizing hormone (LH). Leydig cells are polyhedral in shape, display a large prominent nucleus, an eosinophilic cytoplasm and numerous lipid-filled vesicles.
Rape	In criminal law, rape is a type of sexual assault usually involving sexual intercourse, which is initiated by one or more persons against another person without that person's consent.
	According to the American Medical Association (1995), sexual violence, and rape in particular, is considered the most under-reported violent crime. The rate of reporting, prosecution and convictions for rape varies considerably in different jurisdictions.
Cancer	Cancer (medical term: malignant neoplasm) is a class of diseases in which a group of cells display uncontrolled growth, invasion that intrudes upon and destroys adjacent tissues, and sometimes metastasis, or spreading to other locations in the body via lymph or blood. These three malignant properties of cancers differentiate them from benign tumors, which do not invade or metastasize.
	Researchers divide the causes of cancer into two groups: those with an environmental cause and those with a hereditary genetic cause.
Testosterone	Testosterone is a steroid hormone from the androgen group and is found in mammals, reptiles, birds, and other vertebrates. In mammals, testosterone is primarily secreted in the testes of males and the ovaries of females, although small amounts are also secreted by the adrenal glands. It is the principal male sex hormone and an anabolic steroid.
Breastfeeding	Breastfeeding is the feeding of an infant or young child with breast milk directly from female human breasts (i.e., via lactation) rather than from a baby bottle or other container. Babies have a sucking reflex that enables them to suck and swallow milk. Most mothers can breastfeed for six months or more, without the addition of infant formula or solid food.

Chapter 6. Male Sexual Anatomy and Physiology

Chapter 6. Male Sexual Anatomy and Physiology

Puberty	Puberty is the process of physical changes by which a child's body becomes an adult body capable of reproduction. Puberty is initiated by hormone signals from the brain to the gonads (the ovaries and testes). In response, the gonads produce a variety of hormones that stimulate the growth, function, or transformation of brain, bones, muscle, blood, skin, hair, breasts, and sex organs. Growth accelerates in the first half of puberty and stops at the completion of puberty. Before puberty, body differences between boys and girls are almost entirely restricted to the genitalia. During puberty, major differences of size, shape, composition, and function develop in many body structures and systems. The most obvious of these are referred to as secondary sex characteristics.
Osteoporosis	Osteoporosis is a disease of bones that leads to an increased risk of fracture. In osteoporosis the bone mineral density (BMD) is reduced, bone microarchitecture is deteriorating, and the amount and variety of proteins in bone is altered. Osteoporosis is defined by the World Health Organization (WHO) as a bone mineral density that is 2.5 standard deviations or more below the mean peak bone mass (average of young, healthy adults) as measured by DXA; the term "established osteoporosis" includes the presence of a fragility fracture.
Steroid	A steroid is a type of organic compound that contains a specific arrangement of four cycloalkane rings that are joined to each other. Examples of steroids include the dietary fat cholesterol, the sex hormones estradiol and testosterone, and the anti-inflammatory drug dexamethasone.
BDSM	BDSM is a consensual lifestyle choice, or type of adult roleplay between two or more individuals. The compound acronym, BDSM, is derived from the terms bondage and discipline (B'D), dominance and submission (D's), sadism and masochism (S'M) BDSM includes a wide spectrum of activities, forms of interpersonal relationships, and distinct subcultures. Activities and relationships within a BDSM context are characterized by the fact that the participants usually take on complementary, but unequal roles, thus the idea of consent of both the partners becomes essential.

Chapter 6. Male Sexual Anatomy and Physiology

Chapter 7. Love and Intimacy

Love	Love is the emotion of strong affection and personal attachment. In philosophical context, love is a virtue representing all of human kindness, compassion, and affection. In some religious contexts, love is not just a virtue, but the basis for all being, as in the Roman Catholic phrase, "God is love".
Unrequited love	Unrequited love is love that is not openly reciprocated or understood as such, even though reciprocation is usually deeply desired. The beloved may or may not be aware of the admirer's deep affections. The Merriam Webster Online Dictionary defines unrequited as "not reciprocated or returned in kind." Analysis As the literary selections suggest, the inability to express and fulfill emotional needs may lead to feelings such as depression, low self-esteem, anxiety and rapid mood swings between depression and euphoria.
Love triangle	A love triangle is usually a romantic relationship involving three people. While it can refer to two people independently romantically linked with a third, it usually implies that each of the three people has some kind of relationship to the other two. The relationships can be friendships, romantic, familial (often siblings), or even pre-existing hatred between rivals.
Triangular theory of love	The triangular theory of love is a theory of love developed by psychologist Robert Sternberg. The theory characterizes love within the context of interpersonal relationships by three different components: 1. Intimacy - Which encompasses feelings of closeness, connectedness, and bondedness. 2. Passion - Which encompasses drives that lead to romance, physical attraction, and sexual consummation. 3. Commitment - Which encompasses, in the short term, the decision to remain with another, and in the long term, the shared achievements and plans made with that other.

Chapter 7. Love and Intimacy

Chapter 7. Love and Intimacy

Reinforcement	Reinforcement is a term in operant conditioning and behavior analysis for the process of increasing the rate or probability of a behavior (e.g. pulling a lever more frequently) by the delivery or emergence of a stimulus (e.g. a candy) immediately or shortly after the behavior, called a "response," is performed. The response strength is assessed by measuring frequency, duration, latency, accuracy, and/or persistence of the response after reinforcement stops. Experimental behavior analysts measured the rate of responses as a primary demonstration of learning and performance in non-humans (e.g. the number of times a pigeon pecks a key in a 10-minute session).
Complex	A complex is a core pattern of emotions, memories, perceptions, and wishes in the personal unconscious organized around a common theme, such as power or status (Schultz, D. ' Schultz, S., 2009). Primarily a psychoanalytic term, it is found extensively in the works of Carl Jung and Sigmund Freud. An example of a complex would be as follows: if you had a leg amputated when you were a child, this would influence your life in profound ways, even if you were wonderfully successful in overcoming the handicap.
Abortion	Abortion is the termination of a pregnancy by the removal or expulsion of a fetus or embryo from the uterus, resulting in or caused by its death. An abortion can occur spontaneously due to complications during pregnancy or can be induced, in humans and other species. In the context of human pregnancies, an abortion induced to preserve the health of the gravida (pregnant female) is termed a therapeutic abortion, while an abortion induced for any other reason is termed an elective abortion.
Intimate relationship	An intimate relationship is a particularly close interpersonal relationship, and the term is sometimes used euphemistically for a sexual relationship. The characteristics of an intimate relationship include an enduring behavioral interdependence, repeated interactions, emotional attachment and need fulfillment. Intimate relationships include friendships, dating relationships, spiritual relationships, and marital relationships and there are individual differences in both the quality and quantity of these relationships.
Narcissism	Narcissism is the personality trait of egotism, vanity, conceit, or simple selfishness. Applied to a social group, it is sometimes used to denote elitism or an indifference to the plight of others.

Chapter 7. Love and Intimacy

Chapter 7. Love and Intimacy

The name "narcissism" was coined by Freud after Narcissus who in Greek myth was a pathologically self-absorbed young man who fell in love with his own reflection in a pool.

Self-love

Self-love is the strong sense of respect for and confidence in oneself. It different from narcissism in that as one practices acceptance and detachment, the awareness of the individual shifts and the individual starts to see him or herself as an extension of all there is. Ultimately, the identification of "I" from a personal individual perspective, shifts to "I" from a perspective of consciousness or life being experienced from the perceptual point of view that we call by our individual names.

Jealousy

Jealousy is a secondary emotion and typically refers to the negative thoughts and feelings of insecurity, fear, and anxiety over an anticipated loss of something that the person values, particularly in reference to a human connection. Jealousy often consists of a combination of presenting emotions such as anger, sadness, and disgust. It is not to be confused with envy.

Stalking

Stalking is a term commonly used to refer to unwanted, obsessive attention by individuals (and sometimes groups of people) to others. Stalking behaviors are related to harassment and intimidation. The word "stalking" is used, with some differing meanings, in psychology and psychiatry and also in some legal jurisdictions as a term for a criminal offense.

Chapter 7. Love and Intimacy

Chapter 8. Childhood and Adolescent Sexuality

Family	In human context, a family is a group of people affiliated by consanguinity, affinity, or co-residence. In most societies it is the principal institution for the socialization of children. Extended from the human "family unit" by affinity, economy, culture, tradition, honor, and friendship are concepts of family that are metaphorical, or that grow increasingly inclusive extending to nationhood and humanism.
Oxytocin	Oxytocin is a mammalian hormone that acts primarily as a neuromodulator in the brain. Also known as alpha-hypophamine (α-hypophamine), oxytocin has the distinction of being the very first polypeptide hormone to be sequenced and synthesized biochemically, by Vincent du Vigneaud et al. in 1953.
Puberty	Puberty is the process of physical changes by which a child's body becomes an adult body capable of reproduction. Puberty is initiated by hormone signals from the brain to the gonads (the ovaries and testes). In response, the gonads produce a variety of hormones that stimulate the growth, function, or transformation of brain, bones, muscle, blood, skin, hair, breasts, and sex organs. Growth accelerates in the first half of puberty and stops at the completion of puberty. Before puberty, body differences between boys and girls are almost entirely restricted to the genitalia. During puberty, major differences of size, shape, composition, and function develop in many body structures and systems. The most obvious of these are referred to as secondary sex characteristics.
Contact	In family law, contact is one of the general terms which denotes the level of contact a parent or other significant person in a child's life can have with that child. Contact forms part of the bundle of rights and privileges which a parent may have in relation to any child of the family. Following ratification of the United Nations Convention on the Rights of the Child in most countries, the term "access" was superseded by the term contact.
Sibling	Siblings (also called sibs) are people who share at least one parent. A male sibling is called a brother; and a female sibling is called a sister. In most societies throughout the world, siblings usually grow up together and spend a good deal of their childhood socializing with one another.
BDSM	BDSM is a consensual lifestyle choice, or type of adult roleplay between two or more individuals. The compound acronym, BDSM, is derived from the terms bondage and discipline (B'D), dominance and submission (D's), sadism and masochism (S'M)

Chapter 8. Childhood and Adolescent Sexuality

Chapter 8. Childhood and Adolescent Sexuality

	BDSM includes a wide spectrum of activities, forms of interpersonal relationships, and distinct subcultures.
	Activities and relationships within a BDSM context are characterized by the fact that the participants usually take on complementary, but unequal roles, thus the idea of consent of both the partners becomes essential.
Body image	Body image is a concept used in numerous disciplines, including psychology, medicine, psychiatry, psychoanalysis, philosophy and cultural and feminist studies. In psychology it tends to include one's perceptions, beliefs, and emotional attitudes towards one's body. The concept is used to discuss various pathologies and disorder, such as anorexia nervosa and other eating disorders, Body Dysmorphic Disorder, Body Integrity Identity Disorder and various post-stroke conditions like Somatoparaphrenia, and Unilateral Neglect. Body image problems may also manifest themselves in psychopathologies like Schizophrenia and Cotard Delusion. Although it is often confused with the term body schema, which concerns postural and motor control, it should be clearly distinguished from this latter term.
Abortion	Abortion is the termination of a pregnancy by the removal or expulsion of a fetus or embryo from the uterus, resulting in or caused by its death. An abortion can occur spontaneously due to complications during pregnancy or can be induced, in humans and other species. In the context of human pregnancies, an abortion induced to preserve the health of the gravida (pregnant female) is termed a therapeutic abortion, while an abortion induced for any other reason is termed an elective abortion.
Abstinence	Abstinence is a voluntary restraint from indulging in bodily activities that are widely experienced as giving pleasure. Most frequently, the term refers to Sexual abstinence, or abstention from alcohol or food. The practice can arise from religious prohibitions or practical considerations.

Chapter 8. Childhood and Adolescent Sexuality

Chapter 8. Childhood and Adolescent Sexuality

Sexual orientation	Sexual orientation describes a pattern of emotional, romantic, or sexual attraction to men, women, both genders, neither gender, or another gender. According to the American Psychological Association, sexual orientation is enduring and also refers to a person's sense of "personal and social identity based on those attractions, behaviors expressing them, and membership in a community of others who share them." The consensus among most contemporary scholars in the field is that one's sexual orientation is not a choice. No simple, single cause for sexual orientation has been conclusively demonstrated, but research suggests that it is by a combination of genetic, hormonal, and environmental influences, with biological factors involving a complex interplay of genetic factors and the early uterine environment.

Chapter 8. Childhood and Adolescent Sexuality

Chapter 9. Adult Sexual Relationships

Dating	Dating is a form of human courtship consisting of social activities done by two persons with the aim of each assessing the other's suitability as a partner in an intimate relationship or as a spouse. While the term has several senses, it usually refers to the act of meeting and engaging in some mutually agreed upon social activity in public, together, as a couple. The protocols and practices of dating, and the terms used to describe it, vary considerably from country to country.
Patriarchy	Patriarchy is a social system in which the role of the male as the primary authority figure is central to social organization, and where fathers hold authority over women, children, and property. It implies the institutions of male rule and privilege, and is dependent on female subordination.
	Historically, the principle of patriarchy has been central to the social, legal, political, and economic organization of Celtic, Germanic, Roman, Greek, Hebrew, Arabian, Indian, and Chinese cultures, and has had a deep influence on modern civilization.
Cancer	Cancer (medical term: malignant neoplasm) is a class of diseases in which a group of cells display uncontrolled growth, invasion that intrudes upon and destroys adjacent tissues, and sometimes metastasis, or spreading to other locations in the body via lymph or blood. These three malignant properties of cancers differentiate them from benign tumors, which do not invade or metastasize.
	Researchers divide the causes of cancer into two groups: those with an environmental cause and those with a hereditary genetic cause.
Cohabitation	Cohabitation is an arrangement whereby two people decide to live together on a longterm or permanent basis in an emotionally and/or sexually intimate relationship. The term is most frequently applied to couples who are not married.

Chapter 9. Adult Sexual Relationships

Chapter 9. Adult Sexual Relationships

Common-law marriage	Common-law marriage, informal marriage or marriage by habit and repute, is a form of interpersonal status that is legally recognized in some jurisdictions as a marriage even though no legally recognized marriage ceremony is performed or civil marriage contract is entered into or the marriage registered in a civil registry. A common-law marriage is legally binding in some common law jurisdictions but has no legal consequence in others. In some jurisdictions without true common-law marriages, for example, Hungary, the term "common-law marriage" is used as a synonym for non-marital relationships such as domestic partnership or reciprocal beneficiaries relationship.
Childless	Childless is a term that refers to a person or couple that does not have any children. Some reasons for childlessness include: - infertility or other medical problems - lack of appropriate resources (financial, community, etc) - lack of a partner, or lack of willingness from their partner - advancing age Childfree Some people make a conscious decision to refrain from procreating or adopting children; many such people identify with the label of childfree. Many childfree individuals prefer the term childfree to the term childless, because the suffix "-less" may imply that their lives are lacking in some way, when childfree individuals typically feel that their lives are complete without children.
Prenuptial agreement	A prenuptial agreement, antenuptial agreement, or premarital agreement, commonly abbreviated to prenup or prenupt, is a contract entered into prior to marriage, civil union or any other agreement prior to the main agreement by the people intending to marry or contract with each other. The content of a prenuptial agreement can vary widely, but commonly includes provisions for division of property and spousal support in the event of divorce or breakup of marriage. They may also include terms for the forfeiture of assets as a result of divorce on the grounds of adultery; further conditions of guardianship may be included as well.
Sex change	Sex change in animals

Chapter 9. Adult Sexual Relationships

Chapter 9. Adult Sexual Relationships

	In special circumstances some species, such as the clownfish, are known to change sex including reproductive functions. A school of clownfish is always built into a hierarchy with a female fish at the top. When she dies, the most dominant male changes sex and takes her place.
Affair	Affair may refer to professional, personal, or public business matters or to a particular business or private activity of a temporary duration, as in family affair, a private affair, or a romantic affair. Political affair Political affair may refer to the illicit or scandalous activities of public, such as the Watergate affair, or to a legally constituted government department, for example, the United Nations Department of Political Affairs. Romantic affair A romantic affair, also called an affair of the heart, may refer to sexual liaisons among unwed parties, or to various forms of nonmonogamy.
Same-sex relationship	A same-sex relationship is a relationship between two persons of the same gender and can take many forms, from romantic and sexual, to non-romantic close relationships. The relationship is mainly associated with gay and lesbian people. In their essential psychological respects, these relationships are regarded equivalent to heterosexual relationships.
Civil union	A civil union is a legally recognized union similar to marriage. Civil unions can often come under other terms such as registered partnership and civil partnership. Beginning with Denmark in 1989, civil unions under one name or another have been established by law in many developed countries in order to provide same-sex couples rights, benefits, and responsibilities similar (in some countries, identical) to opposite-sex civil marriage.
Parenting	Parenting is the process of promoting and supporting the physical, emotional, social, and intellectual development of a child from infancy to adulthood. Parenting refers to the activity of raising a child rather than the biological relationship.

Chapter 9. Adult Sexual Relationships

Chapter 9. Adult Sexual Relationships

In the case of humans, it is usually done by the biological parents of the child in question, although governments and society take a role as well.

No-fault divorce | No-fault divorce is a divorce in which the dissolution of a marriage requires neither a showing of wrong-doing of either party nor any evidentiary proceedings at all. Laws providing for no-fault divorce allow a family court to grant a divorce in response to a petition by either party to the marriage, without requiring the petitioner to provide evidence that the respondent has committed a breach of the marital contract. Laws providing for no-fault divorce also limit the potential legal defenses of a respondent who would prefer to remain married.

Chapter 9. Adult Sexual Relationships

Chapter 10. Sexual Expression: Arousal and Response

Rape	In criminal law, rape is a type of sexual assault usually involving sexual intercourse, which is initiated by one or more persons against another person without that person's consent.
	According to the American Medical Association (1995), sexual violence, and rape in particular, is considered the most under-reported violent crime. The rate of reporting, prosecution and convictions for rape varies considerably in different jurisdictions.
Cancer	Cancer (medical term: malignant neoplasm) is a class of diseases in which a group of cells display uncontrolled growth, invasion that intrudes upon and destroys adjacent tissues, and sometimes metastasis, or spreading to other locations in the body via lymph or blood. These three malignant properties of cancers differentiate them from benign tumors, which do not invade or metastasize.
	Researchers divide the causes of cancer into two groups: those with an environmental cause and those with a hereditary genetic cause.
BDSM	BDSM is a consensual lifestyle choice, or type of adult roleplay between two or more individuals. The compound acronym, BDSM, is derived from the terms bondage and discipline (B'D), dominance and submission (D's), sadism and masochism (S'M)
	BDSM includes a wide spectrum of activities, forms of interpersonal relationships, and distinct subcultures.
	Activities and relationships within a BDSM context are characterized by the fact that the participants usually take on complementary, but unequal roles, thus the idea of consent of both the partners becomes essential.

Chapter 10. Sexual Expression: Arousal and Response

Chapter 10. Sexual Expression: Arousal and Response

Blue balls	Blue balls is the slang term for a congested prostate or vasocongestion, the condition of temporary fluid congestion in the testicles and prostate region caused by prolonged sexual arousal in the human male often accompanied by acute testicular pain or testicular congestion due to prolonged and unsatisfied sexual excitement. The term is thought to have originated in the United States, first appearing in 1916. Some urologiosts call the condition "epididymal hypertension".
Celibacy	Celibacy refers to a state of not being married, or a state of abstention from sexual intercourse or vow of marriage. This word derives from two Proto-Indo-European stems, *kaiwelo- "alone" and *lib(h)s- "living". Abstinence and celibacy The words abstinence and celibacy are often used interchangeably, but are different.
Sexual intercourse	Sexual intercourse, commonly refers to the act in which the male reproductive organ enters the female reproductive tract. The two entities may be of opposite sexes, or they may be hermaphroditic, as is the case with snails. The definition may additionally include penetrative sexual acts between same-sex pairings, such as penetration of non-sexual organs (oral intercourse, anal intercourse) or by non-sexual organs (fingering, tonguing), which are also commonly practiced by heterosexual couples.
Missionary	A missionary is a member of a religious group sent into an area to do evangelism or ministries of service, such as education, literacy, social justice, health care and economic development. The word "mission" originates from 1598 when the Jesuits sent members abroad, derived from the Latin missionem (nom. missio), meaning "act of sending" or mittere, meaning "to send".
Love	Love is the emotion of strong affection and personal attachment. In philosophical context, love is a virtue representing all of human kindness, compassion, and affection. In some religious contexts, love is not just a virtue, but the basis for all being, as in the Roman Catholic phrase, "God is love".

Chapter 10. Sexual Expression: Arousal and Response

Chapter 10. Sexual Expression: Arousal and Response

Lesbian	Lesbian is a term most widely used in the English language to describe sexual and romantic desire between females. The word may be used as a noun, to refer to women who identify themselves or who are characterized by others as having the primary attribute of female homosexuality, or as an adjective, to describe characteristics of an object or activity related to female same-sex desire.
Sexual orientation	Sexual orientation describes a pattern of emotional, romantic, or sexual attraction to men, women, both genders, neither gender, or another gender. According to the American Psychological Association, sexual orientation is enduring and also refers to a person's sense of "personal and social identity based on those attractions, behaviors expressing them, and membership in a community of others who share them." The consensus among most contemporary scholars in the field is that one's sexual orientation is not a choice. No simple, single cause for sexual orientation has been conclusively demonstrated, but research suggests that it is by a combination of genetic, hormonal, and environmental influences, with biological factors involving a complex interplay of genetic factors and the early uterine environment.
Oedipus complex	In psychoanalytic theory, the term Oedipus complex denotes the emotions and ideas that the mind keeps in the unconscious, via dynamic repression, that concentrate upon a boy's desire to sexually possess his mother, and kill his father. In the course of his psychosexual development, the complex is the boy's phallic stage formation of a discrete sexual identity; a girl's analogous experience is the Electra complex. The Oedipus complex occurs in the third -- phallic stage (ages 3-6) -- of five psychosexual development stages: (i) the Oral, (ii) the Anal, (iii) the Phallic, (iv) the Latent, and (v) the Genital -- in which the source libido pleasure is in a different erogenous zone of the infant's body.

Chapter 10. Sexual Expression: Arousal and Response

Chapter 11. Sexual Orientation

BDSM	BDSM is a consensual lifestyle choice, or type of adult roleplay between two or more individuals. The compound acronym, BDSM, is derived from the terms bondage and discipline (B'D), dominance and submission (D's), sadism and masochism (S'M)
	BDSM includes a wide spectrum of activities, forms of interpersonal relationships, and distinct subcultures.
	Activities and relationships within a BDSM context are characterized by the fact that the participants usually take on complementary, but unequal roles, thus the idea of consent of both the partners becomes essential.
Triangulation	Triangulation is most commonly used to express a situation in which one family member will not communicate directly with another family member, but will communicate with a third family member, which can lead to the third family member becoming part of the triangle. The concept originated in the study of dysfunctional family systems, but can describe behaviors in other systems as well, including work.
	Triangulation can also be used as a label for a form of "splitting" in which one person plays the third family member against one that he or she is upset about.
Interaction	Interaction is a kind of action that occurs as two or more objects have an effect upon one another. The idea of a two-way effect is essential in the concept of interaction, as opposed to a one-way causal effect. A closely related term is interconnectivity, which deals with the interactions of interactions within systems: combinations of many simple interactions can lead to surprising emergent phenomena.
Therapy	Therapy is the attempted remediation of a health problem, usually following a diagnosis. In the medical field, it is synonymous with the word "treatment". Among psychologists, the term may refer specifically to psychotherapy or "talk therapy".

Chapter 11. Sexual Orientation

Chapter 11. Sexual Orientation

Sexual orientation	Sexual orientation describes a pattern of emotional, romantic, or sexual attraction to men, women, both genders, neither gender, or another gender. According to the American Psychological Association, sexual orientation is enduring and also refers to a person's sense of "personal and social identity based on those attractions, behaviors expressing them, and membership in a community of others who share them." The consensus among most contemporary scholars in the field is that one's sexual orientation is not a choice. No simple, single cause for sexual orientation has been conclusively demonstrated, but research suggests that it is by a combination of genetic, hormonal, and environmental influences, with biological factors involving a complex interplay of genetic factors and the early uterine environment.
Hate crime	Hate crimes (also known as bias-motivated crimes) occur when a perpetrator targets a victim because of his or her perceived membership in a certain social group, usually defined by racial group, religion, sexual orientation, disability, class, ethnicity, nationality, age, gender, gender identity, social status or political affiliation. "Hate crime" generally refers to criminal acts that are seen to have been motivated by bias against one or more of the types above, or of their derivatives. Incidents may involve physical assault, damage to property, bullying, harassment, verbal abuse or insults, or offensive graffiti or letters (hate mail).
Lesbian	Lesbian is a term most widely used in the English language to describe sexual and romantic desire between females. The word may be used as a noun, to refer to women who identify themselves or who are characterized by others as having the primary attribute of female homosexuality, or as an adjective, to describe characteristics of an object or activity related to female same-sex desire.
Passing	Passing refers to a person's ability to be regarded as a member of the sex or gender with which they physically present. Typically, passing involves a mixture of physical gender cues (for example, hair style or clothing) as well as certain behavioral attributes that tend to be culturally associated with a particular gender. Irrespective of a person's presentation, many experienced crossdressers assert that confidence is far more important for passing than the physical aspects of appearance.

Chapter 11. Sexual Orientation

Chapter 11. Sexual Orientation

Homophobia	Homophobia is a range of negative attitudes and feelings towards lesbian, gay, bisexual, and in some cases transgender and intersex people. Definitions refer variably to antipathy, contempt, prejudice, aversion, and irrational fear. Homophobia is observable in critical and hostile behavior such as discrimination and violence on the basis of a perceived non-heterosexual orientation.
Machismo	Machismo is prominently exhibited or excessive masculinity. As an attitude, machismo ranges from a personal sense of virility to a more extreme male chauvinism. The trait may be seen as the product of runaway evolution, as Frits Staal notes, The peacock's tail, the enlarged claw of the male fiddler crab and the machismo of members of the human species are all exaggerated features that may cause injury to individuals that display them but attract females.
Homosexuality	Homosexuality is romantic and/or sexual attraction or behavior among members of the same sex or gender. As a sexual orientation, homosexuality refers to "an enduring pattern of or disposition to experience sexual, affectional, or romantic attractions" primarily or exclusively to people of the same sex; "it also refers to an individual's sense of personal and social identity based on those attractions, behaviors expressing them, and membership in a community of others who share them."
Coming out	Coming out is a figure of speech for lesbian, gay, bisexual, and transgender (LGBT) people's disclosure of their sexual orientation and/or gender identity. Framed and debated as a privacy issue, coming out of the closet is described and experienced variously as: a psychological process or journey; decision-making or risk-taking; a strategy or plan; a mass or public event; a speech act and a matter of personal identity; a rite of passage; liberation or emancipation from oppression; a means toward feeling gay pride instead of shame and social stigma; or even career suicide. Author Steven Seidman writes that "it is the power of the closet to shape the core of an individual's life that has made homosexuality into a significant personal, social, and political drama in twentieth-century America."
Parenting	Parenting is the process of promoting and supporting the physical, emotional, social, and intellectual development of a child from infancy to adulthood. Parenting refers to the activity of raising a child rather than the biological relationship. In the case of humans, it is usually done by the biological parents of the child in question, although governments and society take a role as well.

Chapter 11. Sexual Orientation

Chapter 11. Sexual Orientation

Oedipus complex	In psychoanalytic theory, the term Oedipus complex denotes the emotions and ideas that the mind keeps in the unconscious, via dynamic repression, that concentrate upon a boy's desire to sexually possess his mother, and kill his father. In the course of his psychosexual development, the complex is the boy's phallic stage formation of a discrete sexual identity; a girl's analogous experience is the Electra complex. The Oedipus complex occurs in the third -- phallic stage (ages 3-6) -- of five psychosexual development stages: (i) the Oral, (ii) the Anal, (iii) the Phallic, (iv) the Latent, and (v) the Genital -- in which the source libido pleasure is in a different erogenous zone of the infant's body.
Stigma	Stigma -- is the receptive tip of a carpel, or of several fused carpels, in the gynoecium of a flower. The stigma receives pollen at pollination and it is on the stigma that the pollen grain germinates. The stigma is adapted to catch and trap pollen with various hairs, flaps, or sculpturings.
Heterosexism	Heterosexism is a system of attitudes, bias, and discrimination in favor of opposite-sex sexuality and relationships. It can include the presumption that everyone is heterosexual or that opposite-sex attractions and relationships are the only norm and therefore superior. Although heterosexism is defined in the online editions of the American Heritage Dictionary of the English Language and the Merriam-Webster Collegiate Dictionary as anti-gay discrimination and/or prejudice "by heterosexual people" and "by heterosexuals", people of any sexual orientation can hold such attitudes and bias.
Biphobia	Biphobia is a term used to describe aversion felt toward bisexuality and bisexuals as a social group or as individuals. People of any sexual orientation can experience such feelings of aversion. A source of discrimination against bisexuals, biphobia is based on negative bisexual stereotypes and bisexual erasure.
Bisexuality	Bisexuality is sexual behavior or an orientation involving physical and/or romantic attraction to both males and females. It is one of the three main classifications of sexual orientation, along with a heterosexual and a homosexual orientation, all a part of the heterosexual-homosexual continuum. Individuals who lack sexual attraction to either sex are known as asexual.
Heterophobia	Heterophobia describes reverse discrimination based on sexual orientation and implies an irrational fear of or aversion toward heterosexual people and institutions. Coined as a direct analogy to homophobia, "heterophobia" is used by some opponents to various legal and civil rights for lesbian, gay, bisexual, and transgender (LGBT) people, when is used instead of heterosexism. History of the term

Chapter 11. Sexual Orientation

Chapter 11. Sexual Orientation

	The term heterophobia was included in the Dictionary of Sexuality published in 1995 by American sexologist Robert T. Francoeur, where it was defined as fear of heterosexuals.
Cancer	Cancer (medical term: malignant neoplasm) is a class of diseases in which a group of cells display uncontrolled growth, invasion that intrudes upon and destroys adjacent tissues, and sometimes metastasis, or spreading to other locations in the body via lymph or blood. These three malignant properties of cancers differentiate them from benign tumors, which do not invade or metastasize.
	Researchers divide the causes of cancer into two groups: those with an environmental cause and those with a hereditary genetic cause.
Personality development disorder	Personality development disorder is a concept which is currently discussed in Europe . Personality development disorder is considered to be a childhood risk factor or early stage of a later personality disorder in adulthood. The term personality development disorder is used to emphasize the changes in personality development which might still take place and the open outcome during development.

Chapter 11. Sexual Orientation

Chapter 12. Pregnancy and Birth

BDSM	BDSM is a consensual lifestyle choice, or type of adult roleplay between two or more individuals. The compound acronym, BDSM, is derived from the terms bondage and discipline (B'D), dominance and submission (D's), sadism and masochism (S'M)
	BDSM includes a wide spectrum of activities, forms of interpersonal relationships, and distinct subcultures.
	Activities and relationships within a BDSM context are characterized by the fact that the participants usually take on complementary, but unequal roles, thus the idea of consent of both the partners becomes essential.
Abortion	Abortion is the termination of a pregnancy by the removal or expulsion of a fetus or embryo from the uterus, resulting in or caused by its death. An abortion can occur spontaneously due to complications during pregnancy or can be induced, in humans and other species. In the context of human pregnancies, an abortion induced to preserve the health of the gravida (pregnant female) is termed a therapeutic abortion, while an abortion induced for any other reason is termed an elective abortion.
Sex selection	Parents frequently prefer their offspring to be of a particular sex for a variety of reasons. Social sex selection or human sex selection is the attempt to control the sex of the offspring to achieve a desired sex. It can be accomplished in several ways, both pre- and post-implantation of an embryo, as well as at birth.
Maternity	Maternity is the social and legal acknowledgment of the parental relationship between a mother and her child.
	It is specially related with the protection of the baby and the mother within and after the childbirth.

Chapter 12. Pregnancy and Birth

Chapter 12. Pregnancy and Birth

Family	In human context, a family is a group of people affiliated by consanguinity, affinity, or co-residence. In most societies it is the principal institution for the socialization of children. Extended from the human "family unit" by affinity, economy, culture, tradition, honor, and friendship are concepts of family that are metaphorical, or that grow increasingly inclusive extending to nationhood and humanism.
Parenting	Parenting is the process of promoting and supporting the physical, emotional, social, and intellectual development of a child from infancy to adulthood. Parenting refers to the activity of raising a child rather than the biological relationship. In the case of humans, it is usually done by the biological parents of the child in question, although governments and society take a role as well.
Transfer	Transfer is a technique used in propaganda and advertising. Also known as association, this is a technique of projecting positive or negative qualities (praise or blame) of a person, entity, object, or value (an individual, group, organization, nation, patriotism, etc). to another in order to make the second more acceptable or to discredit it.
Love	Love is the emotion of strong affection and personal attachment. In philosophical context, love is a virtue representing all of human kindness, compassion, and affection. In some religious contexts, love is not just a virtue, but the basis for all being, as in the Roman Catholic phrase, "God is love".
Section	The section of an Alpine club (or that of any such Alpine society or association) is an independent club or society that, together with the other sections, forms the main organisation ("Alpine club"). Membership of an Alpine club is normally only possible through membership of a section. The task of an Alpine club section is the maintenance of tradition and culture, the Alpine training of its members, the planning and implementation of mountain tours and expeditions, and also the maintenance of huts and trails in the mountains.
Engagement	An engagement is a promise to marry, and also the period of time between proposal and marriage - which may be lengthy or trivial. During this period, a couple is said to be affianced, betrothed, engaged to be married, or simply engaged. Future brides and grooms are often referred to as fiancées or fiancés respectively .

Chapter 12. Pregnancy and Birth

Chapter 12. Pregnancy and Birth

Depression	Depression is a state of low mood and aversion to activity that can affect a person's thoughts, behaviour, feelings and physical well-being. It may include feelings of sadness, anxiety, emptiness, hopelessness, worthlessness, guilt, irritability, or restlessness. Depressed people may lose interest in activities that once were pleasurable, experience difficulty concentrating, remembering details, or making decisions, and may contemplate or attempt suicide.
Breastfeeding	Breastfeeding is the feeding of an infant or young child with breast milk directly from female human breasts (i.e., via lactation) rather than from a baby bottle or other container. Babies have a sucking reflex that enables them to suck and swallow milk. Most mothers can breastfeed for six months or more, without the addition of infant formula or solid food.
Cancer	Cancer (medical term: malignant neoplasm) is a class of diseases in which a group of cells display uncontrolled growth, invasion that intrudes upon and destroys adjacent tissues, and sometimes metastasis, or spreading to other locations in the body via lymph or blood. These three malignant properties of cancers differentiate them from benign tumors, which do not invade or metastasize. Researchers divide the causes of cancer into two groups: those with an environmental cause and those with a hereditary genetic cause.

Chapter 12. Pregnancy and Birth

Chapter 13. Contraception and Abortion

Contraception	Contraception are techniques and methods use to prevent human fertilization. Other birth control methods include contragestion, which prevents the implantation of the blastocyst, and abortion, the removal or expulsion of a fetus or embryo from the uterus. The techniques and methods frequently overlap.
BDSM	BDSM is a consensual lifestyle choice, or type of adult roleplay between two or more individuals. The compound acronym, BDSM, is derived from the terms bondage and discipline (B'D), dominance and submission (D's), sadism and masochism (S'M) BDSM includes a wide spectrum of activities, forms of interpersonal relationships, and distinct subcultures. Activities and relationships within a BDSM context are characterized by the fact that the participants usually take on complementary, but unequal roles, thus the idea of consent of both the partners becomes essential.
Lifestyle	Lifestyle is a term to describe the way a person lives, which was originally coined by Austrian psychologist Alfred Adler in 1929. The current broader sense of the word dates from 1961. A set of behaviors, and the senses of self and belonging which these behaviors represent, are collectively used to define a given lifestyle. The term is defined more broadly when used in politics, marketing, and publishing. A lifestyle is a characteristic bundle of behaviors that makes sense to both others and oneself in a given time and place, including social relations, consumption, entertainment, and dress.
Cancer	Cancer (medical term: malignant neoplasm) is a class of diseases in which a group of cells display uncontrolled growth, invasion that intrudes upon and destroys adjacent tissues, and sometimes metastasis, or spreading to other locations in the body via lymph or blood. These three malignant properties of cancers differentiate them from benign tumors, which do not invade or metastasize.

Chapter 13. Contraception and Abortion

Chapter 13. Contraception and Abortion

	Researchers divide the causes of cancer into two groups: those with an environmental cause and those with a hereditary genetic cause.
Abortion	Abortion is the termination of a pregnancy by the removal or expulsion of a fetus or embryo from the uterus, resulting in or caused by its death. An abortion can occur spontaneously due to complications during pregnancy or can be induced, in humans and other species. In the context of human pregnancies, an abortion induced to preserve the health of the gravida (pregnant female) is termed a therapeutic abortion, while an abortion induced for any other reason is termed an elective abortion.
Rape	In criminal law, rape is a type of sexual assault usually involving sexual intercourse, which is initiated by one or more persons against another person without that person's consent. According to the American Medical Association (1995), sexual violence, and rape in particular, is considered the most under-reported violent crime. The rate of reporting, prosecution and convictions for rape varies considerably in different jurisdictions.
Abstinence	Abstinence is a voluntary restraint from indulging in bodily activities that are widely experienced as giving pleasure. Most frequently, the term refers to Sexual abstinence, or abstention from alcohol or food. The practice can arise from religious prohibitions or practical considerations.
Breastfeeding	Breastfeeding is the feeding of an infant or young child with breast milk directly from female human breasts (i.e., via lactation) rather than from a baby bottle or other container. Babies have a sucking reflex that enables them to suck and swallow milk. Most mothers can breastfeed for six months or more, without the addition of infant formula or solid food.
Public opinion	Public opinion is the aggregate of individual attitudes or beliefs held by the adult population. Public opinion can also be defined as the complex collection of opinions of many different people and the sum of all their views.

Chapter 13. Contraception and Abortion

Chapter 13. Contraception and Abortion

The principle approaches to the study of public opinion may be divided into 4 categories:

1. quantitative measurement of opinion distributions;
2. investigation of the internal relationships among the individual opinions that make up public opinion on an issue;
3. description or analysis of the public role of public opinion;
4. study both of the communication media that disseminate the ideas on which opinions are based and of the uses that propagandists and other manipulators make of these media.

Concepts of "public opinion"

Public opinion as a concept gained credence with the rise of "public" in the eighteenth century.

Prolactin

Prolactin is a protein that in humans is encoded by the PRL gene. Prolactin is a peptide hormone discovered by Dr. Henry Friesen, primarily associated with lactation. In breastfeeding, the act of an infant suckling the nipple stimulates the production of oxytocin, which stimulates the "milk let-down" reflex, which fills the breast with milk via a process called lactogenesis, in preparation for the next feed.

Parental consent

Parental consent laws (also known as parental involvement or parental notification laws) in some countries require that one or more parents consent to or be notified before their minor child can legally engage in certain activities.

Chapter 13. Contraception and Abortion

Chapter 13. Contraception and Abortion

Parental consent may refer to:

- A parent's right to give consent, or be informed, before their minor child undergoes medical treatment.
- A parent's right to give consent before their minor child undergoes body modification such as piercing or tattooing.
- A parent's right to consent to their minor child marrying before he or she reaches marriageable age.
- A parent's right to be involved in their minor child's education, including the right to approve or disapprove of certain curricula, or to consent to extracurricular activity and field trips.

Chapter 13. Contraception and Abortion

Chapter 14. Challenges to Sexual Functioning

Female sexual arousal disorder	Female sexual arousal disorder commonly referred to as frigidity, is a disorder characterized by a persistent or recurrent inability to attain sexual arousal or to maintain arousal until the completion of a sexual activity, or an adequate lubrication-swelling response that otherwise is present during arousal and sexual activity. The condition should be distinguished from a general loss of interest in sexual activity and from other sexual dysfunctions, such as the orgasmic disorder (anorgasmia) and hypoactive sexual desire disorder, which is characterized as a lack or absence of sexual fantasies and desire for sexual activity for some period of time. Although female sexual dysfunction is currently a contested diagnostic, pharmaceutical companies are beginning to promote products to treat FSD, often involving low doses of testosterone.
Therapy	Therapy is the attempted remediation of a health problem, usually following a diagnosis. In the medical field, it is synonymous with the word "treatment". Among psychologists, the term may refer specifically to psychotherapy or "talk therapy".
Rape	In criminal law, rape is a type of sexual assault usually involving sexual intercourse, which is initiated by one or more persons against another person without that person's consent. According to the American Medical Association (1995), sexual violence, and rape in particular, is considered the most under-reported violent crime. The rate of reporting, prosecution and convictions for rape varies considerably in different jurisdictions.
BDSM	BDSM is a consensual lifestyle choice, or type of adult roleplay between two or more individuals. The compound acronym, BDSM, is derived from the terms bondage and discipline (B'D), dominance and submission (D's), sadism and masochism (S'M) BDSM includes a wide spectrum of activities, forms of interpersonal relationships, and distinct subcultures.

Chapter 14. Challenges to Sexual Functioning

Chapter 14. Challenges to Sexual Functioning

	Activities and relationships within a BDSM context are characterized by the fact that the participants usually take on complementary, but unequal roles, thus the idea of consent of both the partners becomes essential.
Cancer	Cancer (medical term: malignant neoplasm) is a class of diseases in which a group of cells display uncontrolled growth, invasion that intrudes upon and destroys adjacent tissues, and sometimes metastasis, or spreading to other locations in the body via lymph or blood. These three malignant properties of cancers differentiate them from benign tumors, which do not invade or metastasize. Researchers divide the causes of cancer into two groups: those with an environmental cause and those with a hereditary genetic cause.
Disinhibition	Disinhibition is a term in psychology used to describe a lack of restraint manifested in several ways, including disregard for social conventions, impulsivity, and poor risk assessment. Disinhibition affects motor, instinctual, emotional, cognitive and perceptual aspects with signs and symptoms similar to the diagnostic criteria for mania. Hypersexuality, hyperphagia, and aggressive outbursts are indicative of disinhibited instinctual drives.
Diabetes mellitus	Diabetes mellitus is a group of metabolic diseases in which a person has high blood sugar, either because the body does not produce enough insulin, or because cells do not respond to the insulin that is produced. This high blood sugar produces the classical symptoms of polyuria (frequent urination), polydipsia (increased thirst) and polyphagia (increased hunger).
Incontinence	Incontinence is often used by philosophers to translate the Greek term Akrasia (?κρασ?α). Often used to refer to a lacking in moderation or self-control, especially related to sexual desire. This concept is also called wantonness.
Depression	Depression is a state of low mood and aversion to activity that can affect a person's thoughts, behaviour, feelings and physical well-being. It may include feelings of sadness, anxiety, emptiness, hopelessness, worthlessness, guilt, irritability, or restlessness. Depressed people may lose interest in activities that once were pleasurable, experience difficulty concentrating, remembering details, or making decisions, and may contemplate or attempt suicide.

Chapter 14. Challenges to Sexual Functioning

Chapter 14. Challenges to Sexual Functioning

Major depressive disorder	Major depressive disorder is a mental disorder characterized by an all-encompassing low mood accompanied by low self-esteem, and by loss of interest or pleasure in normally enjoyable activities. This cluster of symptoms (syndrome) was named, described and classified as one of the mood disorders in the 1980 edition of the American Psychiatric Association's diagnostic manual. The term "depression" is ambiguous.
Schizophrenia	Schizophrenia is a mental disorder characterized by a disintegration of thought processes and of emotional responsiveness. It most commonly manifests as auditory hallucinations, paranoid or bizarre delusions, or disorganized speech and thinking, and it is accompanied by significant social or occupational dysfunction. The onset of symptoms typically occurs in young adulthood, with a global lifetime prevalence of about 0.3-0.7%.

Chapter 14. Challenges to Sexual Functioning

Chapter 15. Sexually Transmitted Infections and HIV/AIDS

Latency	Latency is a concept in political science referring to existent political opinions that have yet to be fully expressed. Leaders may arouse latent opinions and convert them into political action.
Rape	In criminal law, rape is a type of sexual assault usually involving sexual intercourse, which is initiated by one or more persons against another person without that person's consent. According to the American Medical Association (1995), sexual violence, and rape in particular, is considered the most under-reported violent crime. The rate of reporting, prosecution and convictions for rape varies considerably in different jurisdictions.
Genital wart	Genital warts (or Condylomata acuminata, venereal warts, anal warts and anogenital warts) is a highly contagious sexually transmitted disease caused by some sub-types of human papillomavirus (HPV). It is spread through direct skin-to-skin contact during oral, genital, or anal sex with an infected partner. Warts are the most easily recognized symptom of genital HPV infection, where types 6 and 11 are responsible for 90% of genital warts cases.
AIDS	Acquired immune deficiency syndrome or acquired immunodeficiency syndrome (AIDS) is a disease of the human immune system caused by the human immunodeficiency virus (HIV). This condition progressively reduces the effectiveness of the immune system and leaves individuals susceptible to opportunistic infections and tumors. HIV is transmitted through direct contact of a mucous membrane or the bloodstream with a bodily fluid containing HIV, such as blood, semen, vaginal fluid, preseminal fluid, and breast milk.
Cancer	Cancer (medical term: malignant neoplasm) is a class of diseases in which a group of cells display uncontrolled growth, invasion that intrudes upon and destroys adjacent tissues, and sometimes metastasis, or spreading to other locations in the body via lymph or blood. These three malignant properties of cancers differentiate them from benign tumors, which do not invade or metastasize. Researchers divide the causes of cancer into two groups: those with an environmental cause and those with a hereditary genetic cause.

Chapter 15. Sexually Transmitted Infections and HIV/AIDS

Chapter 15. Sexually Transmitted Infections and HIV/AIDS

Therapy	Therapy is the attempted remediation of a health problem, usually following a diagnosis. In the medical field, it is synonymous with the word "treatment". Among psychologists, the term may refer specifically to psychotherapy or "talk therapy".
Detection	In general, detection is the extraction of particular information from a larger stream of information without specific cooperation from or synchronization with the sender.
	In the history of radio communications, the term "detector" was first used for a device that detected the simple presence or absence of a radio signal, since all communications were in Morse code. The term is still in use today to describe a component that extracts a particular signal from all of the electromagnetic waves present.

Chapter 15. Sexually Transmitted Infections and HIV/AIDS

Chapter 16. Varieties of Sexual Expression

Paraphilia	Paraphilia is a biomedical term used to describe sexual arousal to objects, situations, or individuals that are not part of normative stimulation and that may cause distress or serious problems for the paraphiliac or persons associated with him or her. A paraphilia involves sexual arousal and gratification towards sexual behavior that is atypical and extreme. The term was coined by Wilhelm Stekel in the 1920s.
Love	Love is the emotion of strong affection and personal attachment. In philosophical context, love is a virtue representing all of human kindness, compassion, and affection. In some religious contexts, love is not just a virtue, but the basis for all being, as in the Roman Catholic phrase, "God is love".
Love triangle	A love triangle is usually a romantic relationship involving three people. While it can refer to two people independently romantically linked with a third, it usually implies that each of the three people has some kind of relationship to the other two. The relationships can be friendships, romantic, familial (often siblings), or even pre-existing hatred between rivals.
Psychoanalytic theory	Psychoanalytic theory refers to the definition and dynamics of personality development which underlie and guide psychoanalytic and psychodynamic psychotherapy. First laid out by Sigmund Freud, psychoanalytic theory has undergone many refinements since his work . Psychoanalytic theory came to full prominence as a critical force in the last third of the twentieth century as part of 'the flow of critical discourse after the 1960s', and in association above all with the name of Jacques Lacan.
Courtship	Courtship is the period in a couple's relationship which precedes their engagement and marriage, or establishment of an agreed relationship of a more enduring kind. In courtship, a couple get to know each other and decide if there will be an engagement or other such agreement. A courtship may be an informal and private matter between two people or may be a public affair, or a formal arrangement with family approval.
Courtship disorder	Courtship disorder is a theoretical construct in sexology in which a certain set of paraphilias are seen as specific instances of anomalous courtship instincts in men. The specific paraphilias are exhibitionism, voyeurism, telephone scatologia, frotteurism, and biastophilia (paraphilic rape). According to the Courtship disorder hypothesis, there is a species-typical courtship process in human males consisting of four phases, and anomalies in different phases result in one of these paraphilic sexual interests.

Chapter 16. Varieties of Sexual Expression

Chapter 16. Varieties of Sexual Expression

Drag	Drag is used for any clothing carrying symbolic significance but usually referring to the clothing associated with one gender role when worn by a person of the other gender. The term may have originated in Athens, Greece in the fourth century BCE. when it was common practice for gender-nonconforming people to be dragged through the streets as punishment. The term "drag" may have been given a wider circulation in Polari, a gay street argot in England in the early part of the 20th century.
Transvestism	Transvestism is the practice of cross-dressing, which is wearing clothing traditionally associated with the opposite sex. Transvestite refers to a person who cross-dresses; however, the word often has additional connotations.
Transgenderism	Transgenderism is a social movement seeking transgender rights and affirming transgender pride. History In her 1995 book Apartheid of Sex, biopolitical lawyer and writer Martine Rothblatt describes "transgenderism" as a grassroots social movement seeking transgender rights and affirming transgender pride. For many in the transgender - or "trans" - movement, the label transgender encompasses not only transsexual and transgender people but also transvestites, drag queens, drag kings, intersex individuals, and anyone non-conventionally gendered (i.e., anyone identifying or behaving in a manner that runs counter to expected societal norms concerning the gender assigned them after birth) or sexed (if one includes transsexual people).
BDSM	BDSM is a consensual lifestyle choice, or type of adult roleplay between two or more individuals. The compound acronym, BDSM, is derived from the terms bondage and discipline (B'D), dominance and submission (D's), sadism and masochism (S'M) BDSM includes a wide spectrum of activities, forms of interpersonal relationships, and distinct subcultures.

Chapter 16. Varieties of Sexual Expression

Chapter 16. Varieties of Sexual Expression

	Activities and relationships within a BDSM context are characterized by the fact that the participants usually take on complementary, but unequal roles, thus the idea of consent of both the partners becomes essential.
Bottom	In BDSM, a bottom is the partner in a BDSM relationship or a BDSM scene who takes the passive, receiving, or obedient role, to that of the top or dominant.
	A bottom can, for example, be subject to acts such as flogging, servitude or humiliation and can be physically restrained by bondage, which can itself be painful. A person who submits control of a large percentage of their day-to-day life to a dominant partner, or who submits within a formal set of rules and rituals is sometimes referred to as a slave to that of the master or mistress.
Voyeurism	In clinical psychology, voyeurism is the sexual interest in or practice of spying on people engaged in intimate behaviors, such as undressing, sexual activity, or other activity usually considered to be of a private nature. In popular imagination the term is used in a more general sense to refer to someone who habitually observes others without their knowledge, with no necessary implication of sexual interest.
	Voyeurism can take several forms, but its principal characteristic is that the voyeur does not normally relate directly with the subject of their interest, who is often unaware of being observed.
Rape	In criminal law, rape is a type of sexual assault usually involving sexual intercourse, which is initiated by one or more persons against another person without that person's consent.
	According to the American Medical Association (1995), sexual violence, and rape in particular, is considered the most under-reported violent crime. The rate of reporting, prosecution and convictions for rape varies considerably in different jurisdictions.

Chapter 16. Varieties of Sexual Expression

Chapter 16. Varieties of Sexual Expression

Personality development disorder	Personality development disorder is a concept which is currently discussed in Europe. Personality development disorder is considered to be a childhood risk factor or early stage of a later personality disorder in adulthood. The term personality development disorder is used to emphasize the changes in personality development which might still take place and the open outcome during development.
Therapy	Therapy is the attempted remediation of a health problem, usually following a diagnosis. In the medical field, it is synonymous with the word "treatment". Among psychologists, the term may refer specifically to psychotherapy or "talk therapy".

Chapter 16. Varieties of Sexual Expression

Chapter 17. Power and Sexual Coercion

Assault	Assault is a crime of violence against another person. In some jurisdictions, including Australia and New Zealand, assault refers to an act that causes another to apprehend immediate and personal violence, while in other jurisdictions, such as much of the United States, assault may refer only to the threat of violence caused by an immediate show of force. Assault is often defined to include not only violence, but any intentional physical contact with another person without their consent.
Rape	In criminal law, rape is a type of sexual assault usually involving sexual intercourse, which is initiated by one or more persons against another person without that person's consent. According to the American Medical Association (1995), sexual violence, and rape in particular, is considered the most under-reported violent crime. The rate of reporting, prosecution and convictions for rape varies considerably in different jurisdictions.
Sexual assault	Sexual assault is an assault of a sexual nature on another person. Although sexual assaults most frequently are by a man on a woman, it may be by a man on a man, woman on a man or woman on a woman, adult on a child, adult on an adult or child on a child. While sexual assaults are associated with the crime of rape, it may cover assaults which would not be considered rape.
Feminist theory	Feminist theory is the extension of feminism into theoretical, or philosophical discourse, it aims to understand the nature of gender inequality. It examines women's social roles and lived experience, and feminist politics in a variety of fields, such as anthropology and sociology, psychoanalysis, economics, literary criticism, and philosophy. While generally providing a critique of social relations, much of feminist theory also focuses on analyzing gender inequality and the promotion of women's rights, interests, and issues.

Chapter 17. Power and Sexual Coercion

Chapter 17. Power and Sexual Coercion

Posttraumatic stress disorder	Posttraumatic stress disorder is a severe anxiety disorder that can develop after exposure to any event that results in psychological trauma. This event may involve the threat of death to oneself or to someone else, or to one's own or someone else's physical, sexual, or psychological integrity, overwhelming the individual's ability to cope. As an effect of psychological trauma, PTSD is less frequent and more enduring than the more commonly seen acute stress response.
Stress	Stress is a term in psychology and biology, first coined in the biological context in the 1930s, which has in more recent decades become commonly used in popular parlance. It refers to the consequence of the failure of an organism - human or animal - to respond appropriately to emotional or physical threats, whether actual or imagined. Signs of stress may be cognitive, emotional, physical or behavioral.
Lesbian	Lesbian is a term most widely used in the English language to describe sexual and romantic desire between females. The word may be used as a noun, to refer to women who identify themselves or who are characterized by others as having the primary attribute of female homosexuality, or as an adjective, to describe characteristics of an object or activity related to female same-sex desire.
Oedipus complex	In psychoanalytic theory, the term Oedipus complex denotes the emotions and ideas that the mind keeps in the unconscious, via dynamic repression, that concentrate upon a boy's desire to sexually possess his mother, and kill his father. In the course of his psychosexual development, the complex is the boy's phallic stage formation of a discrete sexual identity; a girl's analogous experience is the Electra complex. The Oedipus complex occurs in the third -- phallic stage (ages 3-6) -- of five psychosexual development stages: (i) the Oral, (ii) the Anal, (iii) the Phallic, (iv) the Latent, and (v) the Genital -- in which the source libido pleasure is in a different erogenous zone of the infant's body.
Cancer	Cancer (medical term: malignant neoplasm) is a class of diseases in which a group of cells display uncontrolled growth, invasion that intrudes upon and destroys adjacent tissues, and sometimes metastasis, or spreading to other locations in the body via lymph or blood. These three malignant properties of cancers differentiate them from benign tumors, which do not invade or metastasize.

Chapter 17. Power and Sexual Coercion

Chapter 17. Power and Sexual Coercion

	Researchers divide the causes of cancer into two groups: those with an environmental cause and those with a hereditary genetic cause.
Abuse	Abuse is the improper usage or treatment for a bad purpose, often to unfairly or improperly gain benefit, physical or verbal maltreatment, injury, sexual assault, violation, rape, unjust practices; wrongful practice or custom; offense; crime, or otherwise verbal aggression. Abuse can come in many forms.
	Abuses such as verbal abuse and physical abuse can be consensual within the confines of erotic humiliation and BDSM.
	Satanic ritual abuse was simply a moral panic and not substantiated as a credible type of abuse.
Child sexual abuse	Child sexual abuse is a form of child abuse in which an adult or older adolescent uses a child for sexual stimulation. Forms of child sexual abuse include asking or pressuring a child to engage in sexual activities (regardless of the outcome), indecent exposure of the genitals to a child, displaying pornography to a child, actual sexual contact against a child, physical contact with the child's genitals (except in certain non-sexual contexts such as a medical exam), viewing of the child's genitalia without physical contact (except in nonsexual contexts such as a medical exams), or using a child to produce child pornography.
	The effects of child sexual abuse include depression, post-traumatic stress disorder, anxiety, propensity to further victimization in adulthood, and physical injury to the child, among other problems.

Chapter 17. Power and Sexual Coercion

Chapter 17. Power and Sexual Coercion

Incest	Incest is sexual intercourse between close relatives that is illegal in the jurisdiction where it takes place and/or is socially taboo. The type of sexual activity and the nature of the relationship between people that constitutes a breach of law or social taboo vary with culture and jurisdiction. Some societies consider incest to include only those who live in the same household, or who belong to the same clan or lineage; other societies consider it to include "blood relatives"; other societies further include those related by adoption or marriage.
Incest taboo	Incest taboo is a term used by anthropologists to refer to a class of prohibitions, both formal and informal, stated and unstated, against incest, the practice of sexual relations between certain or close relatives, in human societies. There are various theories that seek to explain how and why an incest taboo originates. Some advocates maintain that some sort of incest taboo is universal, while others dispute its universality.
Personality development disorder	Personality development disorder is a concept which is currently discussed in Europe. Personality development disorder is considered to be a childhood risk factor or early stage of a later personality disorder in adulthood. The term personality development disorder is used to emphasize the changes in personality development which might still take place and the open outcome during development.
Sexualization	Sexualization is the act or process of sexualizing. It refers to the making of a person, group or thing to be seen as sexual in nature or a person to become aware of sexuality. It can also refer to the making of an interpersonal relationship into a sexual relationship.
Therapy	Therapy is the attempted remediation of a health problem, usually following a diagnosis. In the medical field, it is synonymous with the word "treatment". Among psychologists, the term may refer specifically to psychotherapy or "talk therapy".
Domestic violence	Domestic violence, spousal abuse, family violence and intimate partner violence(IPV), can be broadly defined as a pattern of abusive behaviors by one or both partners in an intimate relationship such as marriage, dating, family, friends or cohabitation. Domestic violence has many forms including physical aggression (hitting, kicking, biting, shoving, restraining, slapping, throwing objects), or threats thereof; sexual abuse; emotional abuse; controlling or domineering; intimidation; stalking; passive/covert abuse (e.g., neglect); and economic deprivation. Alcohol consumption and mental illness can be co-morbid with abuse, and present additional challenges when present alongside patterns of abuse.
Harassment	Harassment covers a wide range of offensive behaviour. It is commonly understood as behaviour intended to disturb or upset. In the legal sense, it is behaviour which is found threatening or disturbing.

Chapter 17. Power and Sexual Coercion

Chapter 17. Power and Sexual Coercion

Quid pro quo	Quid pro quo indicates a more-or-less equal exchange or substitution of goods or services. English speakers often use the term to mean "a favor for a favor" and the phrases with almost identical meaning include: "what for what", "give and take", "tit for tat", "this for that", and "you scratch my back, and I'll scratch yours".
Sexual harassment	Sexual harassment, is intimidation, bullying or coercion of a sexual nature, or the unwelcome or inappropriate promise of rewards in exchange for sexual favors. In some contexts or circumstances, sexual harassment may be illegal. It includes a range of behavior from seemingly mild transgressions and annoyances to actual sexual abuse or sexual assault.

Chapter 17. Power and Sexual Coercion

Chapter 18. Sexual Images and Selling Sex

Obscenity	An obscenity is any statement or act which strongly offends the prevalent morality of the time, is a profanity, or is otherwise taboo, indecent, abhorrent, or disgusting, or is especially inauspicious. The term is also applied to an object that incorporates such a statement or displays such an act. In a legal context, the term obscenity is most often used to describe expressions (words, images, actions) of an explicitly sexual nature.
Cancer	Cancer (medical term: malignant neoplasm) is a class of diseases in which a group of cells display uncontrolled growth, invasion that intrudes upon and destroys adjacent tissues, and sometimes metastasis, or spreading to other locations in the body via lymph or blood. These three malignant properties of cancers differentiate them from benign tumors, which do not invade or metastasize. Researchers divide the causes of cancer into two groups: those with an environmental cause and those with a hereditary genetic cause.
Rape	In criminal law, rape is a type of sexual assault usually involving sexual intercourse, which is initiated by one or more persons against another person without that person's consent. According to the American Medical Association (1995), sexual violence, and rape in particular, is considered the most under-reported violent crime. The rate of reporting, prosecution and convictions for rape varies considerably in different jurisdictions.
AIDS	Acquired immune deficiency syndrome or acquired immunodeficiency syndrome (AIDS) is a disease of the human immune system caused by the human immunodeficiency virus (HIV). This condition progressively reduces the effectiveness of the immune system and leaves individuals susceptible to opportunistic infections and tumors. HIV is transmitted through direct contact of a mucous membrane or the bloodstream with a bodily fluid containing HIV, such as blood, semen, vaginal fluid, preseminal fluid, and breast milk.

Chapter 18. Sexual Images and Selling Sex

Chapter 18. Sexual Images and Selling Sex

Public opinion	Public opinion is the aggregate of individual attitudes or beliefs held by the adult population. Public opinion can also be defined as the complex collection of opinions of many different people and the sum of all their views. The principle approaches to the study of public opinion may be divided into 4 categories: 1. quantitative measurement of opinion distributions; 2. investigation of the internal relationships among the individual opinions that make up public opinion on an issue; 3. description or analysis of the public role of public opinion; 4. study both of the communication media that disseminate the ideas on which opinions are based and of the uses that propagandists and other manipulators make of these media. Concepts of "public opinion" Public opinion as a concept gained credence with the rise of "public" in the eighteenth century.
BDSM	BDSM is a consensual lifestyle choice, or type of adult roleplay between two or more individuals. The compound acronym, BDSM, is derived from the terms bondage and discipline (B'D), dominance and submission (D's), sadism and masochism (S'M) BDSM includes a wide spectrum of activities, forms of interpersonal relationships, and distinct subcultures. Activities and relationships within a BDSM context are characterized by the fact that the participants usually take on complementary, but unequal roles, thus the idea of consent of both the partners becomes essential.

Chapter 18. Sexual Images and Selling Sex

Chapter 18. Sexual Images and Selling Sex

Bondage	Bondage is the use of restraints for the sexual pleasure of the parties involved. It may be used in its own right, as in the case of rope bondage and breast bondage, or as part of sexual activity or BDSM activity. When a person is sexually aroused by bondage, it may be considered a paraphilia, known as vincilagnia.
Prostitution	Prostitution is the act or practice of providing sexual services to another person in return for payment. People who execute such activities are called prostitutes. Prostitution is one of the branches of the sex industry.
Abortion	Abortion is the termination of a pregnancy by the removal or expulsion of a fetus or embryo from the uterus, resulting in or caused by its death. An abortion can occur spontaneously due to complications during pregnancy or can be induced, in humans and other species. In the context of human pregnancies, an abortion induced to preserve the health of the gravida (pregnant female) is termed a therapeutic abortion, while an abortion induced for any other reason is termed an elective abortion.
Archetype	An archetype is an original model of a person, ideal example, or a prototype upon which others are copied, patterned, or emulated; a symbol universally recognized by all. In psychology, an archetype is a model of a person, personality, or behavior. In philosophy, archetypes since Plato at least, refer to ideal forms of the perceived or sensible things or types.

Chapter 18. Sexual Images and Selling Sex